Alan Bullard

A Light in the Stable

A cantata for Christmas

for SATB choir and organ or piano
with optional soloists, congregation, and with optional small orchestra
or chamber group

MUSIC DEPARTMENT

OXFORD
UNIVERSITY PRESS

Instrumentation

The work may be accompanied in three ways:

1. **With organ or piano**, using the accompaniment printed in the vocal score. The optional Small Bell (in the first movement only) may be played by any available musician.

2. **With chamber group**—1 Fl., 1 Ob., 1 Cl. in B flat/A, 1 Bsn. (or B. Cl.), 1 Tpt. in B flat, 1 Hn. in F (opt.), 1 Perc. (opt.) and 1 Hp. (opt.), together with keyboard (organ or piano). The keyboard part is not the same as that in the vocal score.

3. **With small orchestra**—all the instruments above with the exception of keyboard, together with either string quintet (2 violins, viola, cello, and double bass) or string orchestra.

Instrumental parts and full scores are available to hire from the publisher's Hire Library or appropriate agent.

OXFORD
UNIVERSITY PRESS

Great Clarendon Street, Oxford OX2 6DP, England

Oxford University Press is a department of the University of Oxford.
It furthers the University's aim of excellence in research, scholarship,
and education by publishing worldwide in the UK and in certain other countries

ISBN 978-0-19-340207-2

Printed in Great Britain on acid-free paper by
Halstan & Co. Ltd, Amersham, Bucks.

Contents

Composer's note

A Light in the Stable is designed for church or concert use. The audience or congregation may join in the well-known carols in movements 5 (first verse only), 8, 16, and 19, as indicated, and optional readings are suggested.

The choir parts are designed with some flexibility in mind. They may be sung entirely by SATB choir, but movements 2, 4, 6, 9, 11, 13, and 17 may be sung by soloists, a semi-chorus, or all voices, as shown. Alternatively, these movements may be omitted and replaced by readings, as indicated. Movement 10 can be sung by upper voices (SA) or by SATB. In movements 5 and 14, and optionally in the final two pages of movement 19, there is a soprano part which may be taken either by a solo voice or by a semi-chorus from the main choir. Before the final movement there is a space for a reading and prayers, if desired.

The keyboard part may be played on piano or organ. Organists may wish to omit a few of the RH octave doublings, using the registration to thicken the texture. Pianists may omit the small notes in the LH or, where appropriate, play them in the RH, perhaps an octave higher. Alternatively, some chords may be spread.

Many of the movements can also be performed separately during the Christmas season.

Duration: *c.*35 minutes (without any additional prayers or readings).

Text

The Bible text is taken from the Authorized Version, and this is interspersed with new arrangements of traditional Christmas carols and hymns, and new settings of Christmas texts.

1. Prologue: Of our Maker's love begotten

1. Of our Maker's love begotten,
   Ere the world began to be,
   From Alpha to Omega,
   Stretching to eternity.
   Of the things that are, that have been,
   And that future years shall see,
   Evermore and evermore.

2. By your word was all created,
   You commanded and 'twas done,
   Earth and sky and boundless ocean,
   Universe of Three in One.
   All that sees the moon's soft radiance,
   All that breathes beneath the sun,
   Evermore and evermore.

   Prudentius, trans. J. M. Neale, H. W. Baker,
   and R. F. Davis, altd.

2. The Journey

And it came to pass in those days, that there went out a decree from Caesar Augustus, that all the world should be taxed. And Joseph also went up from Galilee, out of the city of Nazareth, into Judaea, unto the city of David, which is called Bethlehem; to be taxed with Mary his espoused wife, being great with child.

> Luke 2: 1, 4–5 (abridged)

As an alternative to this movement, a reading may be substituted, for example Luke 2: 1–5 (complete).

3. As Joseph was a-walking

1. As Joseph was a-walking,
   He heard an angel sing:
   'This night there shall be born
   On earth our heav'nly King.'

2. 'He neither shall be born
   In mansion nor in hall,
   Nor in the place of Paradise,
   But in an ox's stall.'

3. 'He neither shall be clothed
   In purple nor in pall,
   But all in fair linen
   As wear babies all.'

4. 'He neither shall be rocked
   In silver nor in gold,
   But in a wooden cradle
   That rocks upon the mould.'

5. As Joseph was a-walking,
   He heard an angel sing:
   'This night there shall be born
   On earth our heav'nly King.'

   As Joseph was a-walking.

   English trad., altd.

4. The Shepherds

And there were in the same country shepherds abiding in the fields, keeping watch over their flock by night. And, lo, the angel of the Lord came upon them, and the glory of the Lord shone round about them: and they were sore afraid. And the angel said unto them:

> Luke 2: 8–10a

As an alternative to this movement, a reading may be substituted, for example Luke 2: 8–12.

5. Go tell it on the mountain | While shepherds watched

Go tell it on the mountain
Over the hills and ev'rywhere,
Go tell it on the mountain
That Jesus Christ is born.

1. While shepherds kept their watching
   O'er silent flocks by night,
   Behold, throughout the heavens
   There shone a glorious light.

Go tell it on the mountain (etc.)

2. The shepherds feared and trembled,
   When lo, above the earth
   Rang out the angel chorus
   That hailed our Saviour's birth.

Go tell it on the mountain (etc.)

3. Down in a lonely manger
   The humble Christ was born,
   And God sent us salvation
   That blessed Christmas morn.

Go tell it on the mountain
That Christ is born!

      Trad., compiled by J. W. Work

1. While shepherds watched their flocks by night,
   All seated on the ground,
   The angel of the Lord came down,
   And glory shone around.

2. 'Fear not,' said he (for mighty dread
   Had seized their troubled mind);
   'Glad tidings of great joy I bring
   To you and all mankind.

3. 'To you in David's town this day
   Is born of David's line
   A Saviour, who is Christ the Lord;
   And this shall be the sign:

4. 'The heav'nly Babe you there shall find
   To human view displayed,
   All meanly wrapped in swathing bands,
   And in a manger laid.'

      Nahum Tate, altd.

6. The Angels

And suddenly there was with the angel a multitude of the heav'nly host praising God, and saying:

      Luke 2: 13

As an alternative to this movement, a reading may be substituted, e.g. Luke 2: 13–14.

7. Glory to God in the highest

Glory to God in the highest heav'ns, and on earth peace, goodwill toward all people.
Gloria in excelsis Deo!

      Luke 2: 14, altd.

8. Hark! the herald-angels sing

1. Hark! the herald-angels sing
   Glory to the new-born King;
   Peace on earth and mercy mild,
   God and sinners reconciled:
   Joyful all ye nations rise,
   Join the triumph of the skies,
   With th'angelic host proclaim,
   Christ is born in Bethlehem.
   Hark! the herald-angels sing
   Glory to the new-born King.

2. Christ, by highest heav'n adored,
   Christ, the everlasting Lord,
   Late in time behold him come
   Offspring of a virgin's womb:
   Veiled in flesh the Godhead see,
   Hail th'incarnate Deity!
   Pleased as man with us to dwell,
   Jesus, our Emmanuel.
   Hark! the herald-angels sing
   Glory to the new-born King.

3. Hail the heav'n-born Prince of Peace!
   Hail the Sun of Righteousness!
   Light and life to all he brings,
   Ris'n with healing in his wings;
   Mild he lays his glory by,
   Born that we no more may die,
   Born to raise us from the earth,
   Born to give us second birth.
   Hark! the herald-angels sing
   Glory to the new-born King.

Charles Wesley, altd.

9. The Manger

And Mary, having brought forth her first-born son, wrapped him in swaddling clothes, and laid him in a manger; because there was no room for them at the inn.

Luke 2: 7 (altd.)

As an alternative to this movement, a reading may be substituted, for example Luke 2: 7.

10. The Little Lord Jesus

1. Away in a manger, no crib for a bed,
   The little Lord Jesus laid down his sweet head;
   The stars in the bright sky looked down where he lay,
   The little Lord Jesus asleep on the hay.

2. The cattle are lowing, the baby awakes,
   But little Lord Jesus no crying he makes.
   I love thee, Lord Jesus! Look down from the sky,
   And stay by my side until morning is nigh.

3. Be near me, Lord Jesus; I ask thee to stay
   Close by me for ever, and love me, I pray.
   Bless all the dear children in thy tender care,
   And fit us for heaven, to live with thee there.

19th-century American trad.

11. The shepherds visit the stable

And the shepherds said to one another: Let us now go even unto Bethlehem and see this thing which has come to pass. They found Mary, and Joseph, and the babe lying in a manger. And they glorified and praised God for all the things they had seen.

Luke 2: 15–16, 20 (abridged)

As an alternative to this movement, a reading may be substituted, for example Luke 2: 15–17, 20.

12. He is born (*Il est né*)

He is born, the holy child,
Bagpipers pipe, merry fiddlers play;
He is born, the holy child,
Jesus Christ, come to us today.

Il est né, le divin enfant,
Jouez hautbois, résonnez musettes;
Il est né, le divin enfant,
Chantons tous son avènement.

1. Countless centuries have passed
   Since the prophets announced his coming,
   Countless centuries have passed;
   Now our Saviour is come at last.

1. Depuis plus de quatre mille ans,
   Nous le promettaient les prophètes,
   Depuis plus de quatre mille ans,
   Nous attendions cet heureux temps.

He is born (etc.)

Il est né (etc.)

2. He is gentle, meek, and mild,
   Perfect in grace, with radiant beauty,
   He is gentle, meek, and mild;
   Calmly sleeps the Holy Child.

He is born (etc.)

3. Cradled in a cattle stall,
   Friendly beasts around him lowing;
   Cradled in a cattle stall,
   Precious gift of God to all.

He is born (etc.)

4. Heav'n and earth are joined in one
   By this child of mighty power,
   Heav'n and earth are joined in one;
   Welcome to God's glorious Son!

He is born, the Son of God,
Bagpipers pipe, merry fiddlers play;
He is born, the Son of God,
Jesus Christ, come to us today!

2. Ah! qu'il est beau, qu'il est charmant,
   Ah! que ses grâces sont parfaites!
   Ah! qu'il est beau, qu'il est charmant,
   Qu'il est doux, ce divin enfant!

Il est né (etc.)

3. Une étable est son logement,
   Un peu de paille est sa couchette,
   Une étable est son logement,
   Pour un Dieu quel abaissement!

Il est né (etc.)

4. O Jésus, roi tout puissant,
   Si petit enfant que vous êtes,
   O Jésus, roi puissant,
   Régnez sur nous entièrement!

Il est né, le divin enfant,
Jouez hautbois, résonnez musettes;
Il est né, le divin enfant,
Chantons tous son avènement!

French trad., trans. A.B.

13. Mary ponders these things in her heart

And all they that heard it wondered at those things that were told them by the shepherds. But Mary kept all these things, and pondered them in her heart.

Luke 2: 18–19

As an alternative to this movement, a reading may be substituted, for example Luke 2: 18–19.

14. Sing lullaby!

1. Sing lullaby!
   Lullaby baby, now reclining,
   Sing lullaby!
   Hush, do not wake the Infant King.
   Angels are watching, stars are shining
   Over the place where he is lying:
   Hush, do not wake the Infant King.

3. Sing lullaby!
   Lullaby baby, now a-dozing,
   Sing lullaby!
   Hush, do not wake the Infant King.
   Soon comes the cross, the nails, the piercing,
   Then in the grave at last reposing:
   Hush, do not wake the Infant King.

2. Sing lullaby!
   Lullaby baby, now a-sleeping,
   Sing lullaby!
   Hush, do not wake the Infant King.
   Soon will come sorrow with the morning,
   Soon will come bitter grief and weeping:
   Hush, do not wake the Infant King.

4. Sing lullaby!
   Lullaby! is the babe awaking?
   Sing lullaby!
   Hush, do not wake the Infant King.
   Dreaming of Easter, gladsome morning,
   Conqu'ring death, its bondage breaking:
   Hush, do not wake the Infant King.

Sabine Baring-Gould

8

15. The wise men

Behold, there came wise men from the east to Jerusalem, saying, 'Where is he that is born King of the Jews? for we have seen his star in the east, and are come to worship him.' When Herod the king had heard these things, he was troubled, and he said: 'Go and search diligently for the young child; and when ye have found him, bring me word again, that I may come and worship him also.' And the wise men, being warned of God in a dream that they should not return to Herod, they departed; and, lo, the star, which they saw in the east, went before them, till it came and stood over where the young child was. When they saw the star, they rejoiced with exceeding great joy.

Selected from Matthew 2: 1–3, 8–10, 12

16. As with gladness men of old

1. As with gladness men of old
   Did the guiding star behold,
   As with joy they hailed its light,
   Leading onward, beaming bright,
   So, most gracious God, may we
   Evermore be led to thee.

2. As with joyful steps they sped
   To that lowly manger-bed,
   There to bend the knee before
   Thee, whom heav'n and earth adore,
   So may we with willing feet
   Ever seek thy mercy-seat.

3. As they offered gifts most rare
   At that manger plain and bare,
   So may we with holy joy,
   Pure, and free from sin's alloy,
   All our costliest treasures bring,
   Christ, to thee our heav'nly King.

4. Holy Jesus, ev'ry day
   Keep us in the narrow way;
   And, when earthly things are past,
   Bring our ransomed souls at last
   Where they need no star to guide,
   Where no clouds thy glory hide.

5. In the heav'nly country bright
   Need they no created light;
   Thou its light, its joy, its crown,
   Thou its sun which goes not down:
   There for ever may we sing
   Alleluias to our King.

William Chatterton Dix, altd.

17. The wise men offer their gifts

And when they were come into the house, they saw the young child with Mary his mother, and fell down, and worshipped him: and when they had opened their treasures, they presented unto him gifts; gold, and frankincense, and myrrh.

Matthew 2: 11

As an alternative to this movement, a reading may be substituted, for example Matthew 2: 11.

18. A Light for Today

1. A light in the stable, a light for today:
   A heavenly marvel, this joyous birth;
   The Son of God in a bed of hay,
   The child, who on this sacred day
   Brings a kingdom that stretches from heaven to earth.
   A light in the stable so bare; a light for today.

2. The wise men's gifts lie at Jesus' feet:
   The gold a tribute to a King,
   The frankincense, with its odour sweet,
   Drifts heav'nwards in the rising heat,
   The myrrh for the body's burying.
   A light in the stable so bare; a light for today.

3. And Mary wonders and bows her head,
   And sits as still as a statue of stone;
   Her heart is troubled yet comforted,
   Remembering what the angel had said
   Of an endless reign, and of David's throne.
   A light in the stable so bare; a light for today.

from *Three Kings came a-riding,*
Henry Wadsworth Longfellow, altd.

19. Of our Maker's love begotten

1. Of our Maker's love begotten,
   Ere the world began to be,
   From Alpha to Omega,
   Stretching to eternity.
   Of the things that are, that have been,
   And that future years shall see,
   Evermore and evermore.

2. By your word was all created,
   You commanded and 'twas done,
   Earth and sky and boundless ocean,
   Universe of Three in One.
   All that sees the moon's soft radiance,
   All that breathes beneath the sun,
   Evermore and evermore.

3. O that time for ever blessed,
   When the Virgin, full of grace,
   Brought to birth our holy Saviour,
   Light for all the human race.
   And this babe, the world's Redeemer,
   First revealed his sacred face,
   Evermore and evermore.

4. You, the one of whom the prophets
   Spoke in ages long gone by,
   Now to all the earth revealed,
   As your Name we glorify.
   Shining now, the long-expected,
   Let us loud hosannas cry,
   Evermore and evermore.
   (Noel, noel, for evermore!)

5. Sing, ye heights of heav'n, in praises,
   Angels and archangels sing!
   Wheresoever we are gathered,
   Let our joyful anthems ring.
   Ev'ry tongue your Name confessing,
   Countless voices answering,
   Evermore and evermore!
   (Noel, noel, for evermore!)

Prudentius, trans. J. M. Neale, H. W. Baker,
and R. F. Davis, altd.

for Philip Brunelle and VocalEssence, Minneapolis, USA

A Light in the Stable
A cantata for Christmas

ALAN BULLARD

1. Prologue: Of our Maker's love begotten

Prudentius (348–*c*.410)
trans. J. M. Neale (1818–66), H. W. Baker (1821–77),
and R. F. Davis (1866–1937), altd.

DIVINUM MYSTERIUM
Melody from *Piae Cantiones* (1582)
arr. Alan Bullard

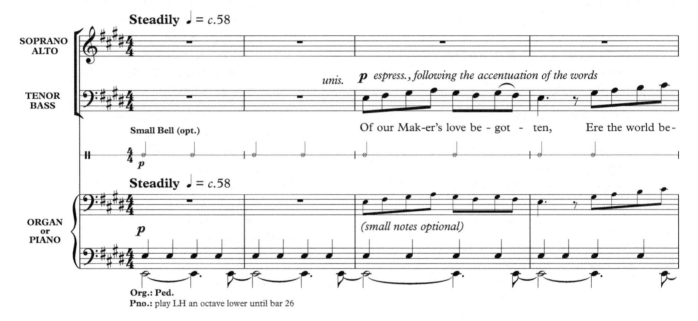

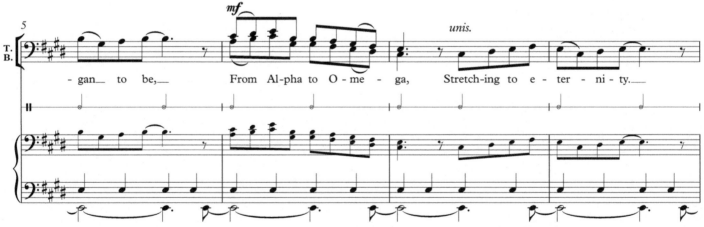

This work may be accompanied either by organ or piano alone, with optional Small Bell in the Prologue only (using this score), or by small orchestra or chamber group, as follows:
1 Fl., 1 Ob., 1 Cl. in B flat/A, 1 Bsn. (or B. Cl.), 1 Tpt. in B flat, 1 Hn. in F (opt.), 1 Perc. (opt.), and 1 Hp. (opt.), together with **either** string quintet, **or** string orchestra, **or** keyboard (organ or piano). The full score and set of parts (including keyboard) are available on hire from the Publisher's Hire Library or appropriate agent.

OXFORD UNIVERSITY PRESS, MUSIC DEPARTMENT, GREAT CLARENDON STREET, OXFORD OX2 6DP
The Moral Rights of the Composer have been asserted. Photocopying this copyright material is ILLEGAL.

9

p

Of the things that are, that have_____ been, And that fu-ture years shall see, Ev-er-more and ev-er-more.___

unis.

13

mp espress., following the accentuation of the words

S./A. *unis.*

mf

S.
A.

By your word was all cre-at - ed,____ You com-mand-ed and_ 'twas done,___ Earth and

mp

T.
B.

_____ By your word was all cre-at - ed, You com-mand-ed and_ 'twas done,

(p)

17

unis.

mp

sky and bound-less o - cean,___ U - ni-verse of Three in One.___ All that sees the moon's soft ra -

mf

mp

unis.

Earth and sky and bound-less o - cean, U - ni-verse of Three in One. All that sees the moon's soft ra -

attacca

2. The Journey*

Luke 2: 1, 3–5 (abridged)

Freely and expressively ♩ = *c.*72

S./A. SOLO, SMALL GROUP, or TUTTI

And it came to pass in those days,___ that there went out a de-cree from Cae-sar Au - gus - tus,___ that all the

T./B. SOLO, SMALL GROUP, or TUTTI

world___ should be taxed.___ And Jo-seph al - so went up from Ga-li-lee, out of the

ci - ty of Na-za-reth, in - to Ju-dae - a,___ un - to the ci - ty of Da - vid, which is called Beth - le -

A little slower

S./A. SOLO, SMALL GROUP, or TUTTI

- hem;___ to be taxed with Ma - ry his e-spous-ed wife, be - ing great___ with child.

attacca

* As an alternative to this movement, a reading may be substituted, for example Luke 2:1–5 (complete)

3. As Joseph was a-walking

English trad., altd.

Alan Bullard

Gently lilting, dream-like ♩ = c.96

1. As Jo - seph was a - walk - ing, He heard an an-gel sing: 'This night there shall be born On earth our heav'n - ly King.'

2. 'He nei - ther shall be born In man - sion nor in hall, Nor in the place of

Pa - ra - dise,____ But in an ox - 's stall.'____ 3. 'He

nei - ther shall be clothed In pur - ple nor in pall, But all in fair lin - en As wear ba - bies

all.'____

But in a wood-en

But in a

4. 'He nei - ther shall be rocked In sil - ver nor in gold,

Man.

(Man.)   Ped.

* Some basses to sing low D, if possible

4. The Shepherds*

Luke 2: 8–10a

* As an alternative to this movement, a reading may be substituted, for example Luke 2: 8–12

5. Go tell it on the mountain | While shepherds watched

Trad., compiled by J. W. Work (1872–1925)
Nahum Tate (1652–1715) altd.

African-American Spiritual
WINCHESTER OLD, Este's *Whole Book of Psalms* (1592)
arr. Alan Bullard

Note: Audience / congregation sing (optionally) in verse 1 of 'While shepherds watched' only, seated

watch-ing O'er si-lent flocks by night, Be-hold, through-out the hea-vens There

Suddenly faster ♩ = c.120

shone a glo-rious light. (TUTTI)

Go tell it on the moun-tain, O-ver the hills and

Go tell it on the mount, go tell it on the moun-tain and

Go tell it on the moun-tain, O-ver the hills and

Suddenly faster ♩ = c.120

SOPRANO SOLO or SEMI-CHORUS

rit. **Relaxed** ♩ = c.108

ev-'ry-where, Go tell it on the moun-tain That Je-sus Christ is born.

ev-'ry-where, Go tell it on the moun-tain, ah

ev-'ry-where,

rit. **Relaxed** ♩ = c.108

p sempre legato

Man.

(Man.)

* *divisi if sung by a group*

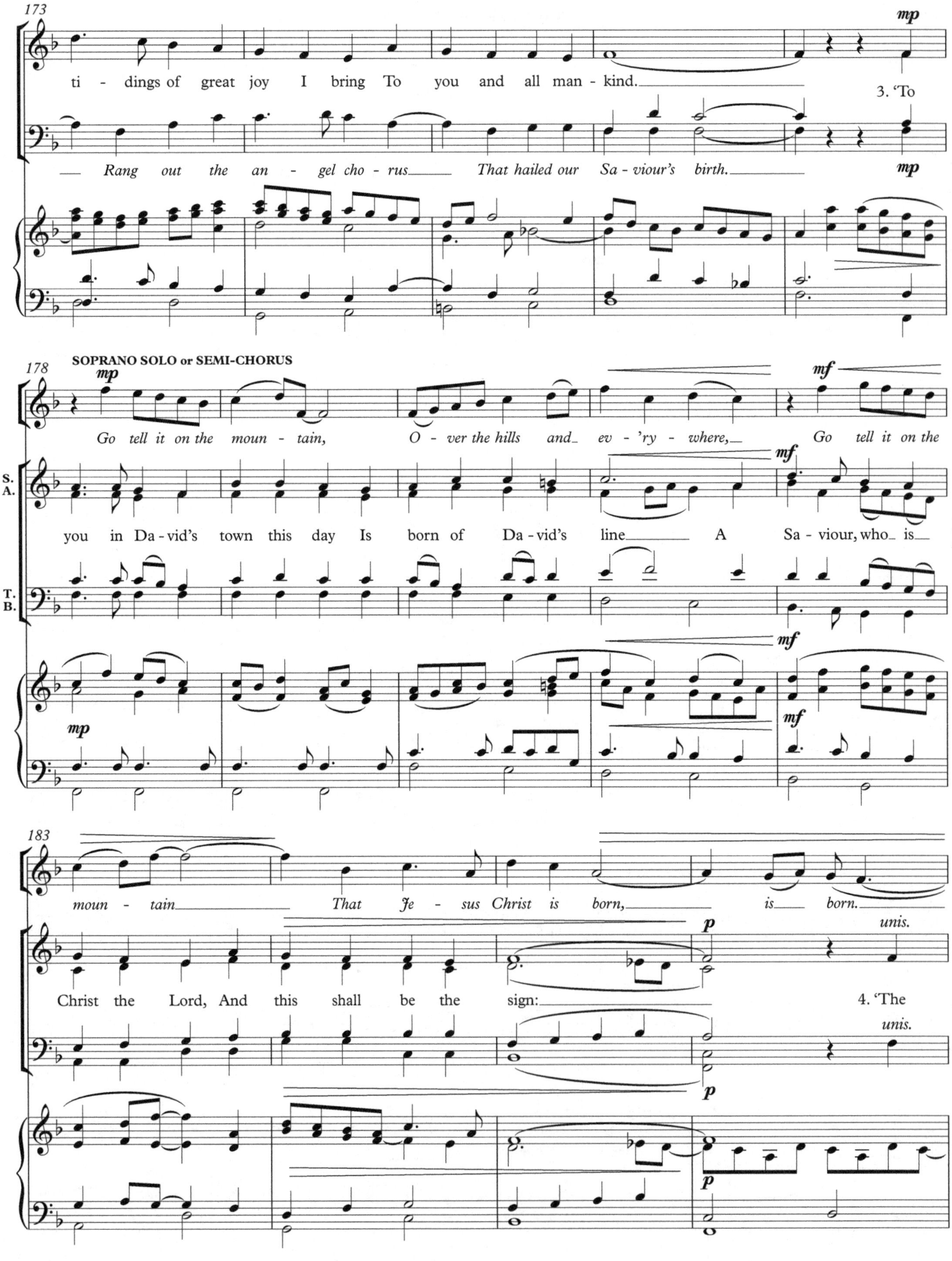

173
mp
ti - dings of great joy I bring To you and all man - kind.
3. 'To
Rang out the an - gel cho - rus That hailed our Sa - viour's birth.
mp
178
SOPRANO SOLO or SEMI-CHORUS
mp
Go tell it on the moun - tain, O - ver the hills and ev - 'ry - where, Go tell it on the
mf
S.
A.
you in Da - vid's town this day Is born of Da - vid's line A Sa - viour, who is
T.
B.
mf
mp
mf
183
moun - tain That Je - sus Christ is born, is born.
p
unis.
Christ the Lord, And this shall be the sign:
4. 'The
unis.
p
p

* Small notes are an alternative option when sung by solo voice; semi-chorus should sing the lower part only

6. The Angels*

Luke 2: 13

* As an alternative to this movement, a reading may be substituted, for example Luke 2: 13–14

7. Glory to God in the highest

Luke 2: 14, altd.

Alan Bullard

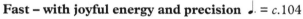

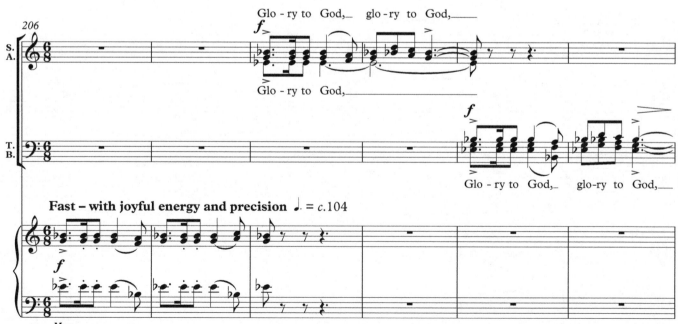

Glo-ry to God in the high - est, glo-ry to God in the high - est, glo-ry to God, glo-ry to God,

God, _____ glo-ry to God in the high - est, glo-ry to God _ on high, glo-ry to God, glo-ry to

Glo - ri - a in ex - cel - sis, glo - ri - a in ex - cel - sis De - - o! _____

God, Glo - ri - a in ex - cel - sis, _____

Pno.: *Ped.*

attacca

8. Hark! the herald-angels sing

MENDELSSOHN
Felix Mendelssohn (1809–47)
adap. William H. Cummings (1831–1915)
vv. 2 & 3 arr. Alan Bullard

Charles Wesley (1707–88) altd.

328

Christ is__ born in Beth-le-hem. *Hark! the he-rald - an-gels sing__ Glo-ry__ to the new-born King.*

334

2. Christ, by high-est heav'n a-dored,__ Christ, the ev-er-last-ing Lord, Late in time be-

339

-hold him come____ Off-spring of a vir-gin's womb: Veiled in flesh the God-head see,__

Hail th'in-car-nate De-i-ty!___ Pleased as man with us to dwell, Je-sus, our Em-

-ma-nu-el. *Hark! the he-rald-an-gels sing___ Glo-ry___ to the new-born King.*

SOPRANO DESCANT

3. Hail the heav'n-born Prince of Peace! Hail the Sun of Right-eous-ness! Light and life to

ALL OTHER VOICES

3. Hail the heav'n-born Prince of Peace! Hail the Sun of Right-eous-ness! Light and life to

9. The Manger*

Luke 2: 7, altd.

Freely

S. /A. SOLO, SMALL GROUP, or TUTTI

And Ma-ry, hav-ing brought forth her first - born son, wrapped him in swad-dling clothes, — and laid him in a man-ger; be-cause there was no room— for them at the inn.

* As an alternative to this movement, a reading may be substituted, for example Luke 2: 7

10. The Little Lord Jesus†

19th-cent. American trad.

James R. Murray (1841–1905) (vv. 1 & 3)
W. J. Kirkpatrick (1838–1921) (vv. 2 & 3)
arr. Alan Bullard

Flowing, and not too slowly ♩ = c.96

S. or S./A. *unis.* or SOLO

1. A - way in a man - ger, no crib for a bed, The lit - tle Lord

A. or T./B. *unis.* or SOLO

Man.

Je - sus laid down his sweet head; The stars in the bright sky looked down where he

† This movement may be sung by either SA or SATB

34

* Optional *divisi*; lower notes must be sung

11. The shepherds visit the stable*

Luke 2: 15–16, 20

* As an alternative to this movement, a reading may be substituted, for example Luke 2: 15–17, 20

36

12. He is born
(*Il est né*)

French trad., tr. A.B. *

French trad.
arr. Alan Bullard

* The original French words are provided as an alternative.
† *divin* pronounced *di-veen*

Since the pro-phets an-nounced his com-ing, Count-less cen - tu - ries have passed; Now our Sa-viour is come at
Nous le pro - met-taient les pro-phè - tes, De-puis plus de qua-tre mille ans, *Nous at - ten-dions cet heu-reux*

last._____ He is born, the_ ho - ly child, Bag - pip-ers pipe, mer-ry
temps._____ Il est né, le di - vin en - fant, Jou - ez haut-bois, ré - son-

fid-dl-ers play;___ He is born, the_ ho - ly child, Je - sus_Christ, come to us to - day.
- nez_ mu - set - tes; Il est né, le di - vin en - fant, Chan - tons_ tous son a - vè - ne - ment.

506
ho - ly child, Je - sus Christ, come to us to - day. 3. Cra - dled in a cat - tle stall,
-vin en - fant, Chan - tons tous son a - vè - ne - ment. 3. Une é - ta - ble est son loge - ment,

p molto legato

511
Friend-ly beasts a - round him low - ing; Cra-dled in a cat - tle stall, Pre-cious gift of
Un peu de paille est sa cou - chet - te, Une é - ta - ble est son loge - ment, Pour un Dieu quel a -

516
God to all. He is born, the ho - ly child, Bag-pip-ers pipe, mer-ry
-bais - se - ment! Il est né, le di - vin en - fant, Jou - ez haut-bois, ré - son-

13. Mary ponders these things in her heart*

Luke 2: 18–19

*As an alternative to this movement, a reading may be substituted, for example Luke 2: 18–19

14. Sing lullaby!

Sabine Baring-Gould (1834–1924)

Alan Bullard

* In the *divisi* sections, Bass 2 may omit the small notes if necessary, joining Bass 1 on the upper notes

comes the cross, the nails, the pierc - ing, Then in the

Comes the cross, the nails, the pierc - ing,

grave at last re - pos - ing:____ 4. Sing lul - la - by! Lul - la - by,

Hush, hush, hush, do not wake the In-fant King.____

Ped.

Man.

15. The wise men

selected from Matthew 2: 1–3, 8–10, 12

Alan Bullard, based on fragments of *We Three Kings*,
J. W. Hopkins (1820–91)

52

attacca

16. As with gladness men of old

DIX

William Chatterton Dix (1837–98) altd.

Abridged from a chorale, *Treuer Heiland*,
by C. Kocher (1786–1872), arr. Alan Bullard

+ AUDIENCE / CONGREGATION in unison

With joy ♩ = c.108

f 1. As with glad-ness men of old
mf 3. As they of-fered gifts most rare

(double choir)

Did the guid-ing star be-hold, As with joy they hailed its light, Lead-ing on-ward, beam-ing bright,
At that man-ger plain and bare, So may we with ho-ly joy, Pure, and free from sin's al-loy,

v. 4: optionally without organ/piano

So, most gra-cious God, may we Ev-er-more be led to thee. *mf* 2. As with joy-ful steps they sped
f All our cost-liest trea-sures bring, Christ, to thee our heav'n-ly King. *p* 4. Ho-ly Je-sus, ev-'ry day

To that low-ly man-ger-bed, There to bend the knee be-fore Thee, whom heav'n and
Keep us in the nar-row way; And, when earth-ly things are past, Bring our ran-somed

earth a - dore,_ So_ may_ we_ with_ will - ing feet___ Ev - er_ seek_ thy_ mer - cy - seat.
souls at last__ Where they_ need no_ star_ to guide,___ Where no_ clouds thy_ glo - ry hide.

SOPRANO DESCANT

5. In the heav'n-ly coun-try bright Need they no_ cre - at - ed light; Thou its_light, its_ joy, its_ crown,

ALL OTHER VOICES

5. In the heav'n-ly coun-try bright Need they no cre - at - ed light; Thou its_light, its_ joy, its_ crown,

Thou its_ sun_ which goes not down. There for ev - er may we sing__ Al - le - lu - ias_ to our_ King.

Thou its_ sun which goes not down. There for ev - er may we sing__ Al - le - lu - ias to our King.

poco rit.

17. The wise men offer their gifts*

Matthew 2: 11

Simply and freely ♩ = c.72

SOLO, SMALL GROUP, or TUTTI

And when they were come in-to the house, they saw the young child with Ma — ry his

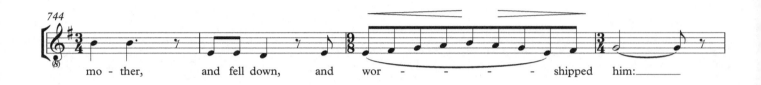

mo - ther,   and fell down,   and wor — — — shipped him:_____

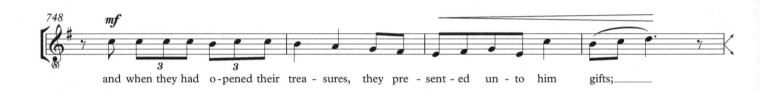

and when they had o-pened their trea - sures, they pre - sent - ed un - to him   gifts;_____

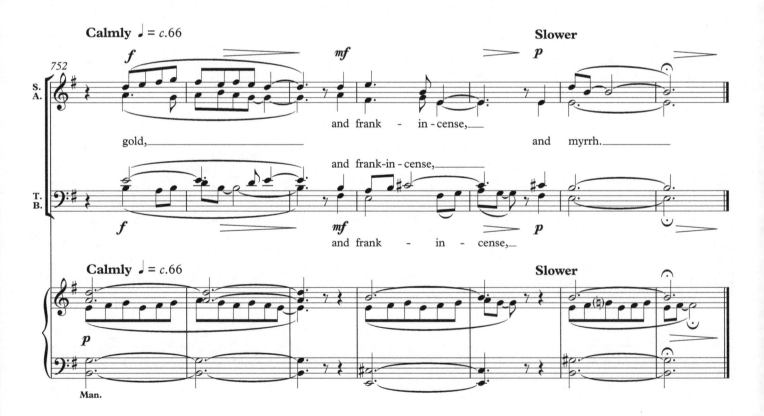

Calmly ♩ = c.66   **Slower**

gold,_____   and frank - in -cense,_____   and   myrrh._____

and frank-in - cense,_____

and frank - in - cense,_____

Man.

* As an alternative to this movement, a reading may be substituted, for example Matthew 2: 11

18. A Light for Today

from *Three Kings came a-riding*
Henry Wadsworth Longfellow (1807–82) altd.

Alan Bullard, based on DIVINUM MYSTERIUM
Melody from *Piae Cantiones* (1582)

* Organ or piano may optionally double the choir throughout this movement

-mem-ber-ing what the an-gel had said Of an end-less reign, and of Da-vid's throne.

ah_____ An end-less reign, and of Da-vid's, Da-vid's

ah_____ An end-less reign, and of Da-vid's, Da-vid's

A light in the sta-ble so bare; *rit.*

throne. A light in the sta-ble, sta-ble so bare; a light,_ a light_for to-day.

throne. A light in the sta-ble bare;

Optional READING, for example John 1: 1–14, and/or optional PRAYERS

19. Of our Maker's love begotten

Prudentius (348–c.410)
tr. J. M. Neale (1818–66), H. W. Baker (1821–77),
and R. F. Davis (1866–1937), altd.

DIVINUM MYSTERIUM
Melody from *Piae Cantiones* (1582)
and a fragment from *The First Nowell*, Anon. English,
arr. Alan Bullard

Joyful and dance-like ♩. = c.80

CHOIR + AUDIENCE / CONGREGATION in unison

1. Of our Mak-er's love be - got-ten,

Ped. *ad lib.*

Ere the world be - gan_ to be, From_ Al - pha to O - me - ga, Stretch-ing to e - ter - ni - ty.

Ped.

Of the things that are, that have_____ been, And that fu-ture years shall see, Ev-er-more and ev-er - more._

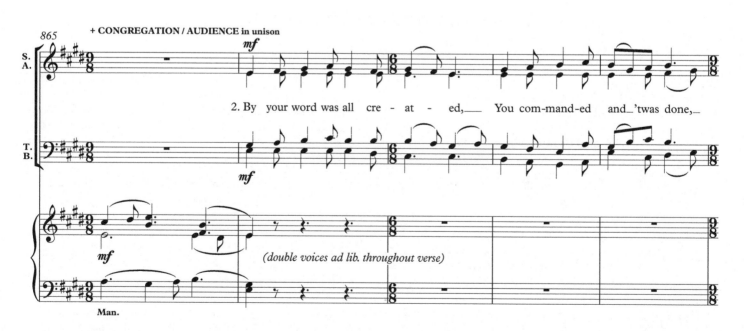

+ CONGREGATION / AUDIENCE in unison

mf

S.
A.

2. By your word was all cre - at - ed,___ You com-mand-ed and_'twas done,___

T.
B.

mf

mf

(double voices ad lib. throughout verse)

Man.

* optional *divisi*

S./A. *unis.* **+ CONGREGATION / AUDIENCE (upper voices only) in unison with S.**

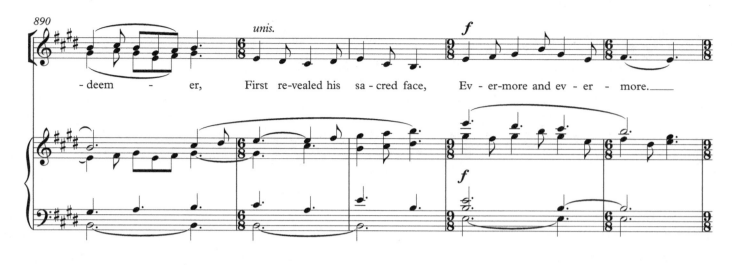

-deem - er, First re-vealed his sa - cred face, Ev - er-more and ev - er - more.____

T./B. *unis.* **+ CONGREGATION / AUDIENCE (lower voices only) in unison with B.**

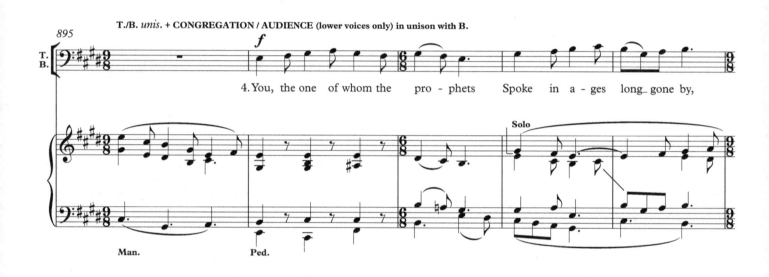

4. You, the one of whom the pro - phets Spoke in a - ges long gone by,

Man.   Ped.

No - el,____ no -

Now to all the earth re - veal - ed, As your Name we glo - ri - fy. Shin-ing now, the long - ex-

Christmas 2013